10

SECRETS TO
A BESTSELLER
WORKBOOK

Other Books by Tim McConnehey

10 Secrets to a Bestseller: An Author's Guide to Self-Publishing

IZZARD INK PUBLISHING COMPANY
PO Box 522251
Salt Lake City, Utah 84152
www.izzardink.com

LIBRARY OF CONGRESS CONTROL NUMBER: 2016908934

Designed by Alissa Rose Theodor
Cover Design by Andrea Ho
Cover Illustration Image Copyright © David van der Veen / Offset.com

First Edition March 2018

Contact the author at info@izzardink.com

Paperback ISBN: 978-1-64228-004-3
e-book ISBN: 978-1-64228-003-6

PRAISE FOR
TIM MCCONNEHEY AND
IZZARD INK PUBLISHING

I have worked with the world's leading multinational companies for my books, in addition to managing my many speaking engagements. Izzard Ink's consultation services were some of the best. I am especially grateful for the guidance with my website and social media marketing campaigns. Izzard Ink's focus is on building authors and people. I would recommend Izzard Ink to any published or non-published author, regardless of where they are in the process.

—Dan Clark, *New York Times* bestselling author of *The Art of Significance*,
National Speaker Association Hall of Fame

My husband, W. Cleon Skousen, wrote several books, including The Naked Communist *and* The Naked Capitalist. *We were so happy when each of those became bestsellers. I was told that, at last count, those two books had sold more than two million copies combined. I've had Izzard Ink refresh five of Cleon's books, and all of them turned out crisp and new and attractive.*

—Jewel P. Skousen, editor and spouse of *USA Today* and *New York Times*
bestselling author W. Cleon Skousen

I am a self-publishing author/publisher and have had the best experience, bar none, with the Izzard Ink group. They are the best bunch of hardworking professionals that I have ever had the privilege of working with; I would recommend them to anyone looking to design a cover or create a beautiful interior; I would recommend them for all your creative publishing needs. Tim McConnehey has held my hand through the entire process and answered my questions at all hours of the day and night. I couldn't be more pleased with the results.

—Diane Merrill Wigginton, author and owner of Jeweled Dagger Publishing

I owe my new friends at Izzard Ink a tremendous debt of gratitude. They walked me through self-publishing 101 and helped me turn my non-sellers into great sellers. One title was a bestseller on Amazon. Until I met Izzard, I didn't know how little I knew about post-writing development to produce a polished, professional-looking book. They cared about making me a success. And where some prior efforts produced a couple of duds, they guided me to help so I could repair the flaws and try again. It was worth it. Highly recommend Izzard Ink. Sometimes you just need somebody who knows the way.

—Paul Skousen, bestselling author and former White House CIA analyst

PRAISE FOR *10 SECRETS TO A BESTSELLER: AN AUTHOR'S GUIDE TO SELF-PUBLISHING*

I got the idea from the book that McConnehey is saying, "If you want to live in a palace, let's draw up the blueprints and start picking out bricks. We can build your palace the way you want it." He wants to keep authors in a place to direct their own decisions, while providing all the help they may need to get the job done.

—Reviewed by Elizabeth White for AML

He makes a great statement that is very true for a writer when he says: "Success is mastering failure." The writer needs to make writing like a job, pick a time to sit down and write. Make yourself do it and accomplish your goals. He also explains how the writer must make the book interesting to the reader, causing them to fall in love with the writer. He gives some terrific insights concerning big publishing companies. There are pros and cons on both sides of the coin, and he shares both sides with the reader.

—Reviewed by Darin Godby for Readers' Favorite

10

SECRETS TO A BESTSELLER

An Author's Guide to
Self-Publishing

TIM McCONNEHEY

IZZARD INK
PUBLISHING

CONTENTS

F I R S T . . .

This workbook is intended to help you define your goals for your book and identify what you need to make your book successful. You probably have dozens of questions about the whole process. This step-by-step inventory will guide you to those important answers.

At Izzard Ink, we want to support your book project to success and share with you part of our process that has helped sell hundreds of thousands of books. In order for us to best help you, to best manage your book through the publication process and to support it in the marketplace, we have created this workbook to help both you and us understand your book project in the greatest possible detail—your goals, your history, what you have in hand, what you want as your final product, and most importantly, how to get there!

If at any point you want to work with a publishing consultant or have questions, please contact Izzard Ink at info@izzardink.com. You can also call us at 415-889-6100. We find that this completed workbook will give you an edge in picking your team and executing your publishing goals.

We strongly suggest that you use this workbook along with *10 Secrets to a Bestseller: An Author's Guide to Self-Publishing*, available through Izzard, to get the most out of the questions and exercises.

Name:_____

Email: _____

Telephone(s): _____

Other contact info (WhatsApp, Skype, etc.):_____

_____

Other (website, Facebook and/or LinkedIn, Pinterest, etc.):_____

_____

Manuscript title:_____

Pen name or publishing name:_____

What is your book about?_____

_____

_____

Length (in words): _____

Genre (for example: fiction, informative, children's, romance, etc.): _____

_____

Has this manuscript been published before?_____

Have you published any books before?_____

Publication details:

What are your goals for this book? Examples might be: to become a public speaker, to market a business, to prove expertise, to provide instruction, as a hobby, or as a commercial enterprise:_____

_____

Is it a series:_____   Do you want to brand it?_____

What is your budget for this book?_____

What is your time frame?_____

_____

Do Your Research

Industry Best Practices

1. Determine your book's genre and audience.

2. Research your market and competition.

Understanding where you fit in the market is an important part of being successful with your book. And the first step in understanding that is to understand the genre and any subgenres your book might belong to. If we wanted to classify our companion book, *10 Secrets to a Bestseller*, we could do so just like a biologist classifies a new species of plant:

- **Domain:** Publishing

- **Kingdom**: Book

- **Phylum:** Instructional

- **Class:** Guide

- **Order:** How-to

- **Family:** Collaborative publishing

- **Genus:** Publish a Bestseller

- **Species:** *10 Secrets to a Bestseller: An Author's Guide to Self-Publishing*

A breakdown for a different kind of book might look like this:

- **Domain:** Publishing

- **Kingdom:** Book

- **Phylum:** Series

- **Class:** Guidebook

- **Order:** Wildlife identification

- **Family:** Birds
- **Genus:** How to Identify series
- **Species:** *Birds of Bali*

And yet again:

- **Domain:** Business/corporate publication
- **Kingdom:** Pamphlet/short e-book
- **Phylum:** Not applicable
- **Class:** Self-help
- **Order:** Personal improvement
- **Family:** Nutrition
- **Genus:** Time Management
- **Species:** *Eating Right for Better Time Management*

How would you classify your book?

(Not all categories may be applicable.)

- **Domain:** _____
- **Kingdom:** _____
- **Phylum:** _____
- **Class:** _____
- **Order:** _____
- **Family(ies:)** _____
- **Genus:** _____
- **Species:** _____

A useful thing to know is how popular and/or unique your book project may be. Using the information above, and researching if you need to, name up to five books in your genre. Your genre, in the above exercise, would be the broad category to which your book belongs; in our examples, they are how-to, guidebook, and self-help, respectively. Go to a bookstore if you need to—it won't be a wasted trip.

1. _____

2. _____

3. _____

4. _____

5. _____

What makes your book unique and different from others in the

genre? _____

_____

_____

_____

Who is your audience? _____

_____

_____

_____

Another good thing to check is whether any books in your genre are on any bestseller lists. *The New York Times*, Amazon, Barnes & Noble, and *USA Today* all have bestseller lists worth looking at. Knowing whether you have a popular topic, or whether the market is saturated or in need, is valuable information when planning your book project.

Are there any books in your genre on any of these lists?

_____

Are there multiple books in your specific genre on any of these lists?

_____

Sometimes you want to be unique in your area, but other times it pays to capitalize on a trend or an event that will help make your book successful. Are there any events or trends that could help sell your book? (For example, with the launch of the Hubble Space Telescope, the hobby of astronomy and building a telescope became very popular, generating hundreds of books, pamphlets, articles, and products.)

_____

_____

_____

My Action Plan

Provide basic book information; classify your book; research market and competition. Make any additional notes here.

_____

_____

_____

_____

_____

_____

_____

_____

_____

_____

_____

_____

Complete Your Manuscript Rough Draft

Industry Best Practices

1. Create a table of contents and/or outline.

Very likely, the hardest thing you will ever do is complete your manuscript. Typically, you will start by completing a rough draft, or a version that you know you will need to review, edit, and rework, even before turning it over to an editor or writing coach. Sometimes you have to plow through places where it's pretty tough going, but the value of a rough draft is that once you have the framework in place, you can go back and smooth over those rough spots.

Sometimes people contact a publisher or agent with a full manuscript; sometimes they just have an idea. Often, they have something in between—a proposal, consisting of the idea; a chapter outline; and possibly a sample of the writing.

How far are you in your rough draft? (Choose one.)

☐ My manuscript is complete.

☐ I have completed a big portion of my manuscript. I estimate it is _____% complete.

☐ I have a little bit written, but not as much as half.

☐ I have an outline.

☐ I have an outline and some of the book. I estimate the manuscript is _____% complete.

☐ I have an idea.

☐ Other:_____

What is the structure of your book? (Examples could be: Your book is set up in chapters; it has thirty chapters; it is in sections and subsections, etc.) If possible, provide the table of contents in the next blank section.

_____

_____

_____

_____

_____

Table of contents of your book:

_____

_____

_____

_____

_____

_____

_____

_____

_____

If you are struggling to complete your manuscript, you may find this section valuable; if not, you can skip to the next section.

Can you outline your book? Use this page to create a chapter-by-chapter or detailed outline.

_____

_____

_____

_____

_____

_____

_____

_____

_____

_____

_____

_____

_____

What is preventing you from completing your manuscript? (For example: research needed, time needed, writer's block, plot holes, going the wrong direction, etc.)

_____

_____

If you encounter frequent writer's block, struggle with plot holes, or face structural issues that keep you from progressing, you might consider working with a writing coach.

If time and money are the problem, consider a grant or a crowdfunding effort. Some grants and awards are specifically geared toward helping writers with their living costs while they are working on projects. Some can help with publishing costs. You might be able to find grants or contests that are intended to help with your type of project or situation—grants for genres, like mystery, science fiction, or nonfiction; local grants for local writers; grants for parents of minor children.

You stated before that the genre of your book is _____ .

Your location (state, province, region, country) is _____ .

Is there anything about your book or your life that might qualify you, specifically, for a grant? Consider things like where you graduated college, your life situation, and your demographics: age, gender, ethnicity, religion, etc. For example, if you are a single father in the Asian community in the U.S., you might find grants specific to single parents or Asian-Americans.

_____

_____

_____

_____

Look for grants online, but don't forget your local library, where you can find resources such as the Foundation Center's publications (and its online service, Foundation Directory Online).

Online, look for GrantSelect to help search for grants by keyword, but beware: A costly subscription is required. If you are a student or instructor, or if your work organization uses grants, check with your institution to see if they have a subscription available for your use.

Using these resources, identify three grants you could apply for:

1. _____

Requirements: _____

_____

_____

2. _____

Requirements: _____

_____

3. _____

Requirements: _____

_____

_____

My Action Plan

Outline the book or create a table of contents to guide the writing; find resources if needed. Make any additional notes here.

_____

_____

_____

_____

_____

_____

_____

_____

_____

_____

_____

_____

_____

Copy and Content Editing

Industry Best Practices

1. Edit for structure, content, and grammar/usage, typically in that order.
2. Fact-check and product-test when content calls for it (technical, cookbooks, historical fiction, nonfiction, etc.).

In *10 Secrets to a Bestseller*, we discuss the editing process used by traditional publishing houses. Authors can expect to have at least two full rounds of editing on their books, including a line edit from a copy editor and a proofread of the final book.

Developmental Editor: In some cases, you might work very closely with a specialized type of editor. A developmental editor, as the name suggests, helps you to develop the content of your manuscript. A developmental editor, in part, looks at your book from your audience's point of view. They may act as a structure editor as well, to ensure that the structure and flow of your book work as intended. Sometimes you might need to work with a writing coach or developmental editor to finish your manuscript.

Content Editor/Fact Checker: If your book makes factual claims, is instructional, or contains something that needs testing, such as recipes for a cookbook, you may need some extra editorial support from a content editor or fact checker to ensure your content is credible.

Specialists: Historical fiction writers, too, might need a specialist to ensure that the book is free from anachronisms—and science fiction authors, don't underestimate your audience. They are more likely than most to know if you're fudging your physics. A technical editor may be needed if you are producing a manual for programming in JavaScript, to ensure your code or your instructions work as claimed.

In traditional book publishing, there are typically three phases of editing that happen in the following order:

Content Edit: The editor focuses on macro elements of the story, such as plot, pacing, character, setting and voice. Often, the editor will write an overarching letter to the author, evaluating the manuscript as a whole. Content editing can include development, structural editing, fact and technical checking, or other work performed by a subject-matter expert.

Line Edit: An editor makes changes at the line level to the language of the story, generally to make it read better, catch inconsistencies and repetitive issues in syntax. The number of changes is entirely dependent on the manuscript—some require heavy line edits and some do not. (It pays to polish it yourself if you are averse to seeing that red pen all over your manuscript.)

Copyedit: A copy editor looks at the very granular elements of grammar, usually ensuring the manuscript aligns with "house style" or a standard such as *The Chicago Manual of Style*. Generally, the person doing copyediting is different from the person who does content and line editing, and he or she is the last stop for quality assurance before reaching the formatter—the person who will prepare the book for publishing.

You may or may not need certain types of content editing, but you can assume you will at least need a line or copy editor—someone to make sure your work is grammatically correct, punctuated, and free from typos.

A manuscript review can help you determine the most appropriate editing path for your book. Consider having a trial edit done to see how you work with an editor and to get a sense of the results. Your Izzard project manager can help you arrange either of these highly recommended options.

To help you make the right choices regarding content editing, check all of the following that apply:

☐ I need professional help to finish my book. *(Content editor or coach)*

☐ My book needs improvement. *(Developmental editor)*

☐ My book needs structural editing. *(Content editor or subject-matter expert)*

☐ My book is nonfiction, factual material. *(Fact checker or subject-matter expert)*

☐ My book requires instructions *(computer code, recipes, etc.)* that need to be confirmed. *(Fact checker or subject-matter expert)*

☐ My book contains computer code examples. *(Technical checker with subject-matter expertise)*

☐ My book is historical fiction. *(Fact checker)*

☐ My book is science fiction. *(Fact checker)*

☐ My book is just fine as it is. *(Content editor and proofreader)*

Remember that it is a good idea to have a line or copy editor look at your book in all cases.

Many people using publishing services have to make choices among these services based on what is affordable. Sometimes one editor can provide more than one service. Using the above list, rate your editing needs by priority—that is, in order of how much value they might bring to your book:

1. _____

2. _____

3. _____

4. _____

5. _____

With this information in hand, you can work more effectively with your Izzard project manager to determine the right type and amount of editing to give your book its best chance at success.

Editing Costs

To get an idea of editing costs, check sites like this one to help compare the quotes you get to a real-live cost model:

https://www.the-efa.org/rates/

And for an inside look at the wide range of services and rates:

https://www.writersmarket.com/assets/pdf/How_Much_Should_I_Charge.pdf

Editing Scheduling

Most good editors are booked at least 2-3 months out at any given time. Sometimes it can be as much as 6 months. Think about starting the hiring process at least a few months in advance to avoid too much lag time.

My Action Plan

I plan to hire the following type(s) of editor:

1. _____

because _____ .

This edit will take place (choose one):

☐ during manuscript development

☐ prior to the final manuscript

☐ after final manuscript completion

2. _____

because _____ .

This edit will take place (choose one):

☐ during manuscript development

☐ prior to the final manuscript

☐ after final manuscript completion

3. _____

because _____ .

This edit will take place (choose one):

☐ during manuscript development

☐ prior to the final manuscript

☐ after final manuscript completion

4. I plan to have a manuscript review: ☐ Yes   ☐ No

5. I plan to have a trial edit: ☐ Yes   ☐ No

Complete Manuscript Final Draft

Industry Best Practices

1. Integrate content and structural editing results into your manuscript.
2. Continue to work with your editor as the manuscript develops.
3. Ask friends and family to read your book and provide input.
4. Have your manuscript proofread.

To finish your final draft, you are going to want to incorporate the feedback from your editor or editors, ensuring it reads smoothly, addresses any questions raised along the way, generally reads the way you want it to, and conveys the message or story you intend to convey.

One strategy for implementing effective changes is to review your manuscript before you dive in with rewrites and corrections, taking note of the types of corrections that repeat and the types of questions your editor asks or struggles with. For instance, consider the following questions:

Do you use a particular word or phrase so often that your editor commented on it, or has to delete or change the same word over and over again? Typical words and phrases that get repeated are: "so," "just," "maybe," "for instance," and similar connecting phrases.

☐ Yes   ☐ No

If yes, what word(s) or phrases do you repeat frequently? _____

Many connecting words or phrases are simply extra and can be deleted. But sometimes you just need another word for the same thing. Using a thesaurus, find three alternatives for each repeated word, and keep this list handy when you work on your final draft.

1. _____

2. _____

3. _____

Did your editor or fact checker find factual errors?

☐ Yes   ☐ No

If yes, research may be required. Sometimes a professional researcher can solve knotty problems for you, particularly in history, science, and technology. If you're writing a book that required research, you're probably pretty tired of looking stuff up by now, but don't shortchange yourself by taking shortcuts. As we will see again and again as we work through the process of publishing your book, shortcuts don't pay off, but an investment in quality almost certainly will.

Did your editor or fact checker find structural errors?

☐ Yes   ☐ No

If yes, you might be looking at a heavy edit. A heavy edit, if you agree with the editor, might result in a heavy rewrite. Don't get discouraged if this is the case—remember that this is the normal process for making a book that people want to read. No one comes out with a bestseller without working hard on that manuscript!

However, the work involved can be intimidating, and you probably feel that you've already put your heart and soul, and a lot of time, into this book. If you're feeling overwhelmed, remember that all jobs can be broken down into smaller steps.

1. Review your editor's work. Go through the entire book and note any questions that you have.

2. Contact your editor to clarify anything that doesn't seem clear to you. Don't be afraid to stay in touch with your editor throughout the final manuscript process, and even to challenge him or her.

3. Break your book down into manageable sections and set a reasonable deadline for each section.

4. If additional work is required, such as research or art permissions, keep a list. Even if you know you'll remember everything on that list, each time you check something off, you get that wonderful "closer-to-done" feeling.

5. If you have problem sections, use a recording device to listen to yourself read that part aloud. Often, when you're reading aloud, the solution to an awkward sentence becomes clear as you read.

6. Use your family and friends—ask them to read your manuscript and give feedback. The more feedback you get from the more types of sources, the more information you have for making the book into the book you wanted it to be.

If you are still struggling, you might need to go back to the basics in your book. Answering the following questions can help you complete your final manuscript.

What is the main thing you wanted to accomplish with your book?

_____

_____

_____

_____

_____

What is the central theme or topic of your book? _____

_____

_____

_____

_____

_____

Rereading your book now, can you identify a central theme?

☐   Yes   ☐   No

Does your book convey that theme in certain terms?

☐   Yes   ☐   No

Does it seem as though your book is saying something other than what you intended? You might see this yourself, or you might derive this from your editor's comments and the reactions of friends and family.

☐   Yes   ☐   No

If you answered "yes" to this question, what message do you think your book unintentionally conveys?

_____

_____

_____

_____

_____

_____

_____

Understanding the difference between what you intended and what you have can serve as a good signpost for getting to where you want to be. But until you can put into words what you intended versus what you have, it will be much harder to move the book in the direction you want.

My Action Plan

Complete the manuscript. Make any additional notes here.

_____

_____

_____

_____

_____

_____

_____

_____

_____

_____

_____

_____

Assemble Your Team

Industry Best Practices

1. Obtain rights for text and image use.
2. Plan what formats in which to release your book.
3. Have a distribution plan for each format.
4. Have a professional designer and/or formatter prepare your book.
5. Get a cover designed by a professional.
6. Create a written marketing plan.

Manuscripting is hard and lonely work. But now that you've gotten this far, the best thing for you and your book is to work with an experienced team that can help you create, assemble, design, and generally prepare your book for a successful release.

As we keep saying at Izzard, successful publishing is a complex process. Many sites offer simple paths to publication that do little more than convert your manuscript into a production format for Kindle or print-on-demand publishing, and then send you on your way. This is a great way to have your book disappear among the thousand other volumes that got published that day.

Have you tried to self-publish your book before? ☐ Yes   ☐ No

If you answered "yes," what was the result? _____

_____

Did you sell any copies?   □ Yes   □ No   How many?_____

If you want your book to have a chance in the market—even if your "market" is a predefined audience, such as the people in your company—you will do yourself a great favor by ensuring that it is as professional as possible in its language, presentation, and distribution. And for this, you need a team of qualified professionals. This statement may sound obvious or expensive or discouraging, but it's important to address. To most writers, the temptation to "do it all" by themselves is a heavily traveled road that leads to anonymity and publishing frustration. You should go the extra mile. Most writers do not. The successful writers do.

Art, Photos, and Illustrations

Certain books, like children's books, cookbooks, nature books, coffee table books, and others, require art. The art might be photographs, as for a biography or volume on history, or they could be illustrations, as for children's books. They might be technical drawings or situational art. Whatever type of art you might be working with, it is important that it both look professional and perform professionally; that is, print or display clearly, cleanly, and—if applicable—legibly.

Creating professional-looking art, more often than not, requires a professional. Translating that art to print or electronic display also requires a professional to ensure that the final result is not fuzzy, poorly cropped, or badly colored.

Image and Text Rights

Many images, particularly photographs (including those found on the internet), have people who own the rights. Using someone else's text when it is not covered by fair-use laws also requires permission before you can put it in your own book. Know what you are using or consider hiring the services of a specialist—it's much cheaper than getting sued later.

Design and Layout

The nice thing about personal computers is that, with a program like Microsoft Word, you can create a rather nice-looking file for your manuscript. The bad thing about personal computers is that, with a program like Microsoft Word, you can create a rather nice-looking file for your manuscript!

The problem is that "rather nice-looking" doesn't usually translate to "professional look and feel." There are more potential pitfalls in design, formatting, and layout than you might expect. Files produced in MS Word and quickly converted to Kindle format using an online service can result in strange line endings and paragraph breaks, titles that blend into text, and other problems that can make it difficult for your readers to read. If you applied design elements to your Word layout, even stranger things can happen in the conversion to electronic format. If you have a complex layout or use devices like columns, lists, illustrations, and so on, they may not translate to the new format.

Even if you are going to print first rather than straight to an e-book, it's important to remember that Word is a word-processing program with a lot of capabilities, but it is not designed for professional publishing. Art can get fuzzy and fonts can get replaced, causing reflow and paging problems.

The result can be unprofessional looking—even unreadable.

The interior of your book should look polished as well: attractive, but not overdesigned. Its job is not to interrupt the reader's experience. Finally, a professional will be able to format for delivery to your desired formats, whether print or electronic—ensuring that the text runs in order and handling text interruptions such as sidebars or other special cases professionally, so that the text flows correctly and that all heads look like heads and all text looks like text in the final products.

Cover Design

The cover is a critical piece of selling your book (see **Marketing**, below), and an amateurish cover can doom your book from the start. Amateur design can also sting you in the area of image rights; even if you are diligent about obtaining rights for the photos in your book, an amateur cover designer might not know the importance of copyright compliance.

Marketing

No matter how excellent your book is, without some attention to marketing, it will get lost. You must make some effort to get your book in front of people who are likely to buy it. Since the majority of authors are not marketing people, Izzard can supply you with the experts who can guide you through the process of deciding when and where to place ads, provide you with ideas on how to get professional reviews, and help you decide how best to promote your book.

Production and Going to Market

You will have to make choices about what formats to publish in: print, e-book, audiobook, and so on. Unless you are a publishing professional yourself, someone will need to prepare your book for these final formats, from text to art to covers. Don't try this at home! Make sure you have professionals on the job.

To help you decide what your book needs to make it successful, the following checklist will help you and your Izzard project manager plan your team right from the beginning.

☐ My book contains art that was specifically drawn for it. (Art can include illustrations, charts and graphs, and other graphic material. Do not include photographs here.)

    ☐ My book contains art that only exists on paper.

    ☐ My book contains art in files of this format(s): _____

    ☐ My book contains art that I got from another source, but I am not sure of the copyright.

    ☐ My book contains art from another source, but I have documentation showing that I have the right to use it, and I have complied with all of its conditions.

    ☐ My book contains color art that will print or display in black and white.

☐ My book contains photographs.

    ☐ My book contains photographs taken by me.

    ☐ My book contains photographs taken by someone I know.

    ☐ My book contains photographs from another source, but I am not sure of the copyright.

    ☐ My book contains photographs from another source, but I have documentation showing that I have the right to use them, and I have complied with all of its conditions.

    ☐ My book contains photographs that only exist on paper.

    ☐ My book contains photographs in this file format(s): _____

    ☐ My book contains color photographs that will print or display in black and white.

☐ My book contains text from another source, such as a complete essay, article, or long passage.

    ☐ My book contains text from another source, but I am not sure of the copyright.

☐ My book contains text from another source, but I have documentation showing that I have the right to use it, and I have complied with all of its conditions.

☐ My book is in this format (e.g., MS Word, Adobe InDesign, paper, etc.):_____

☐ My book has been professionally designed and formatted.

☐ My book needs to be professionally designed and formatted.

☐ My project manager and I feel confident in the cover design.

☐ I need a cover design.

☐ I have a marketing plan in place.

☐ I need help developing a marketing plan.

My Action Plan

I will (choose one)

☐ Hire a professional to figure out rights for my quoted material or borrowed art/photographs.

☐ Perform rights clearance on my own. I will keep careful track of permissions granted in case of future questions.

I plan to publish in the following formats: _____

_____

My distribution plan for each format is: _____

_____

_____

☐ I will hire a professional interior designer and formatter.

☐ I will hire a professional cover designer.

☐ I will create a marketing plan by consulting with my Izzard project manager.

Get Professional Reviews

Industry Best Practices

1. Get at least five professional reviews.

What are professional reviews? They are the reviews that usually end up listed on the cover or inside flap of a printed book. For example, *The Naked Communist,* by W. Cleon Skousen, is published by Izzard and was mentioned on The Glenn Beck Program. Quoting something from Beck's comment is an ideal review because of the reach of his radio program. His many followers will purchase books based solely on his recommendation.

Of course, this is an ideal review scenario, but you too can find qualified people to give you professional reviews. And don't let your personal politics or views stand in the way of a reviewer. You never know who might be listening or reading or watching when your book is mentioned, and want to go read it.

"How?" you are probably asking.

Your first idea may be that you will have to go begging and pleading to get a professional to read and review your book. But in our consulting with authors, the biggest surprise to them is learning that reviews are not only written to help the author, but the reviewer as well.

With *True Stories from the Files of the FBI,* by W. Cleon Skousen, a few of the crimes take place in Chicago. What if we could locate an owner of a business that was somehow related to Chicago crime history? What if they could give a review for the book? A search was done to find a business related to the subject of the book.

We identified Chicago Crime Tours and sought them out for a review. We made arrangements for a personal visit to give Mark Singer of Chicago Crime Tours a copy of the book. After Mark read the book, he sent over an honest review that is now used in all the marketing materials.

Was giving us a review a one-sided deal for Mark Singer and Chicago Crime Tours? Absolutely not. With every book sold, Chicago Crime Tours is listed on the back of the book, which markets their business as well.

They benefit from the mention on various retailer sites, like Amazon and Barnes & Noble. The Chicago Crime Tours brand is listed in the reviews section as well. Along with giving more credibility to *True Stories from the Files of the FBI*, these reviews also give free advertising for Chicago Crime Tours.

Always look for a win/win scenario. Put the interests of others ahead of your own by offering an advantage that will benefit them. It will increase the odds of finding a talented partner to promote your book. This is a great reciprocal agreement that many businesses and professionals can appreciate—an exchange of public relations.

To help you find qualified reviewers, think about the following:

What is the genre of your book? _____

What is the topic of your book? _____

Do you personally know or have a connection to anyone in a field related *in any way* to your genre or topic? If so, list them here.

_____

_____

_____

Has someone else, or several other people, written a book on the same or a parallel subject?

☐ Yes   ☐ No

If yes, name them here. Remember that you will mention their books in the review attribution, so it's free advertising for them.

_____

_____

_____

_____

_____

Is the subject in any way related to a university subject?

☐ Yes   ☐ No   If yes, which subject? _____

List several colleges here. Consider your own college (if you went to one), nearby schools, and community colleges. _____

_____

_____

Using the school's website, find the name of a professor of the subject and a contact phone or email for the professor, his or her department, or the school.

Name:_____

Contact information: _____

What are some tangible aspects of your book that you can name? Include such things as location, the keywords you would use to catalogue it, any public figures mentioned, political viewpoint, intended audience, etc.

_____

_____

_____

Brainstorm some ideas about how these aspects of your book can benefit you. Consider business leaders and businesses in the location setting of your book, people with radio shows with your specialty or point of view, the people you may have mentioned, and so on. And never forget . . . It's free advertising for them, so be daring and creative! Eventually, you will contact people on this list until you have five professional reviews in all.

_____

_____

_____

Using the above worksheet, keep track of your five professional reviewers here:

1. _____

2. _____

3. _____

4. _____

5. _____

My Action Plan

1. Identify aspects of your book that could make for a mutually beneficial connection to a potential reviewer.

2. Identify potential reviewers based on the criterion discussed in this worksheet.

3. Contact your potential reviewers to arrange to send them a copy of your book.

4. Set a time frame for completing the review.

_____

_____

_____

_____

_____

_____

_____

_____

_____

_____

The All-Important Cover

Industry Best Practices

1. Hire a professional designer.

You have the content down for your book. But does the cover pass the seven-second test?

Seven seconds is the average time that potential book buyers will give you to win their attention. A book cover that passes the seven-second test will stand a better chance of being purchased and read. How can you make the most of those seven seconds?

1. You could use a DIY template creator where you upload your own image and title.

2. You could hire a graphic designer.

3. You could make sure that designer is a professional designer with "Big 5 publisher" experience.

You might think that the DIY template looks just fine, and it might, along with thousands of other books whose covers were built using that same template. If you are able to hire a professional cover designer, you won't regret it. A professional will know to execute universally accepted standards that give your book that professional look, especially when creating that all-important first impression that is your cover. A professional will know not to use too many fonts. A professional who specializes in your genre and who is not just a generic graphic designer can tune that cover to appeal specifically to your audience. A professional has learned how colors affect buying decisions, and how they interact with subject matter to attract or repel your reader. And a professional wants the final product to be so outstanding that it will find a place in his or her portfolio to draw in additional clients.

Don't forget about the back cover. Back cover text is perhaps the most critical part of a book for drawing in readers, and too many self-published authors miss this golden opportunity when they publish. The back cover is a great place to grab your reader, with a hook of a headline, teasers from the text, extracts from your professional reviews, and your credentials as a writer and/or expert in your field.

A good designer will make the cover attractive, incorporating front and back text seamlessly. Covers are what make book browsers reach for the book, so this is an area of production you don't want to ignore.

A professional designer knows to start by gathering information. On the next page, a worksheet will walk you through the sorts of information you can expect to have to provide to a professional cover designer.

Typically, the designer will have a title information sheet for you to fill out, providing the details of the book that the designer feels are necessary in order to produce a cover that will really market and sell your book. Include a copy of the book and highlight important sections that you think the designer should know about. And remember to send along those five professional reviews, or as much as you have at this point.

The title information sheet will draw on much of the core information already collected, such as the title and author's name, as well as information specific to the physical book, such as dimensions, and information specific to the book's concept, such as a short summary. An example is provided.

Sample Title Information Sheet

Title: _____

Subtitle: _____

Author's name: _____

BISAC category*: _____

Retail price: _____

ISBN: _____

Page size: _____

---

* BISAC categories are subject codes from the Book Industry Study Group. Codes can be found here: http://bisg.org/page/BISACSubjectCodes

Spine size: _____

Page and/or word count: _____

Brief description: _____

_____

Tag-line description: _____

Book elevator pitch: _____

_____

_____

_____

_____

_____

Three- or four-paragraph description: _____

_____

_____

_____

_____

_____

_____

Author bio: _____

_____

_____

_____

_____

_____

_____

_____

Selling points:

1. _____

_____

2. _____

_____

3. _____

_____

Comparable titles:

1. _____

_____

2. _____

_____

3. _____

_____

Expected audience demographics (age group, gender, etc.):

_____

_____

_____

_____

_____

_____

_____

It is important for the cover designer to understand the style and vision you have for the cover. A trip to your local bookstore or browsing covers online is in order. Jot down a few of your favorite book covers. If you can, narrow the titles down to other books in the same genre as your book.

1. _____

2. _____

3. _____

4. _____

5. _____

6. _____

7. _____

What else do you want the designer to know? Do you have a specific vision or key elements you want included in the cover? Writing down a few of your thoughts will really help the designer understand the direction you want to take.

_____

_____

_____

_____

_____

_____

_____

_____

_____

_____

_____

_____

_____

You will probably receive several design concepts to choose from. Get input from multiple sources, if you can: friends, family, your editor or mentor. Don't forget your Izzard project manager. Listen to their input when selecting which concept to adopt—if you choose any of them. List some people whose opinion would be valuable when selecting a cover concept:

1. _____

2. _____

3. _____

4. _____

5. _____

6. _____

7. _____

My Action Plan

1. Obtain and complete the designer's title information sheet.

2. If not included on the designer's form, write your author bio. (You will need this a lot!)

3. If not included on the form, note any comparable titles and selling points that you would like to bring to the designer's attention.

4. Review the design concepts provided with as many trusted people as possible.

5. Proofread the cover before production.

WORKSHEET VIII.

Going to Retail

Industry Best Practices

1. Deliver to as many platforms as possible.
2. Make available through as many vendors as possible.

Going to retail involves a great many steps. Your manuscript has been or is ready to be formatted, and quality assurance of the final product is one of the major tasks in the final stages of production. Choosing your delivery formats is also a critical part of this step—again, bearing in mind that each delivery format must be thoroughly checked for quality.

Let's start with delivery formats. A book used to be an organized collection of paper that held information or perhaps a story. Now a book can still be that collection of paper, or it can be a digital file or an audio presentation as well. Within the digital world, you can deliver your book to reading devices, or to computer or mobile-device screens, either through reading applications or through the internet.

Printing itself can still be done traditionally, using offset printing, but if you don't know whether your sales will justify a yearly minimum run of 2,500 books, you might be better off using print-on-demand services (POD). POD is growing in popularity because it lets you print a small run as needed for each order, whether it's one at a time or a few hundred. POD may be the best choice for in-house publications, for instance, where the demand is small and changes might be frequent.

E-books offer some functional options that print books can't, such as audio material, video, and hyperlinks. Perhaps most importantly for you, e-books provide a low-cost option, free of the printing and inventory costs that come with traditional print publishing.

Which of the following formats have you thought about or imagined for your book?

☐   Offset print run (you arrange to print a given number of copies, say 2,500, in advance)

☐   Print on demand (you arrange for printing in small batches or on request)

☐   Kindle e-book

☐   Nook e-book

☐   Apple iBook

☐   Other e-book format: _____

☐   Online book (available using an internet application)

☐   Audiobook

Another important question in book production is whether you want to make your book accessible for visually impaired people.

☐   Yes   ☐   No

If yes, the accommodations to be made can vary widely with the content of the book. You and your Izzard project manager will discuss what is required based on your book's needs.

A consideration in e-books is the layout of your book. For some books, a fixed layout is absolutely necessary for the book to make sense, but the default mode for most e-books is to reflow depending on user preferences, such as page size, screen size, type size, font, and other factors beyond your control. (You may be wondering about that wonderful design you have. Rest assured that Izzard's e-books reflect design details like chapter headings, decorations, drop caps, and all those other wonderful details that made your book design pleasing and fresh.) However, if you have a certain type of technical book, or a picture book, or another book in which the layout is part of its fundamental content, you may need to go with a fixed layout. Is that th

☐ Yes   ☐ No

If you require a fixed layout, it may limit somewhat the distribution of your e-book, as not all retailers will accept them. But those won't be the markets your potential readers are browsing, so if a fixed layout is critical to your book, Izzard will make sure that a fixed layout is what you get.

Quality Assurance

In preparation for these delivery formats, you want to make sure that your manuscript file is perfect. If you find a typo later on, you don't want to have to reissue your print book and several different e-books to correct one typo. If an important sentence was dropped, you don't want to have to re-record part of the audiobook. Izzard Ink has a quality-control process that aims to provide the best possible source content for publishing.

In our quality check, we review the following items. You can try to streamline the process by checking for errors and typos within the manuscript yourself, but nothing really substitutes for an experienced typographic proofreader. For one thing, when you and your team have looked at the manuscript so closely for so long, you start to see what you expect to see instead of what is there, leading to possible typos. For another thing, being typographically correct is partly a matter of experience and specialization. Would you be alert to chapters starting on a verso (left-hand) page? Or excessive hyphenation, "rivers" in the text (these are vertically aligned word spaces, which can distract a reader), or orphans and widows?

Izzard's quality check covers the following, at a minimum:

- We check for "widows and orphans." A widow is the last line of a paragraph left on its own at the top of a new page, while an orphan is the first line of a paragraph by itself at the bottom of a page. Traditional typography distinguished the two this way: "An orphan is left behind, whereas a widow must go on alone." Widows and orphans break up the flow of the text, making it more difficult to read.
- We are on the lookout for words accidentally inserted twice.

- We check for proper use of hyphenated line breaks. There should be no more than three lines broken on a hyphen in a row, and preferably no more than two. We also avoid breaking on a word that already contains a hyphen, which creates the distracting double-hyphen effect.

- We make sure the titles and page numbers of the chapters are reflected accurately in the table of contents.

- The running heads at the top of each page might indicate a chapter or section or unit. In the quality check, we ensure the heads reflect the content accurately.

- We check for extra (double) spaces that shouldn't be there.

- We ensure that heads and page numbers are correct. Perhaps chapters should start on the right-hand, or recto, page. This needs to be checked as well.

- In print books, we make sure the flow of text doesn't create unsightly and distracting "rivers," or contiguous gaps, between words.

- We make sure styles are employed consistently and accurately and that they reflect the semantic content.

- We check the spacing of paragraphs and headings to make sure they are consistent throughout the book, with no extra or missing space.

- We compare the original manuscript to the final file to make sure nothing went missing or was changed through the various stages of production.

- We check to ensure that the interior design of the book was properly executed. Are the chapter headings all designed the same way? Are footnotes all spaced correctly? Are the fonts the same as those requested? Do pages' tops and/or bottoms align, as specified in the design?

My Action Plan

1. Make a final decision about which platforms to publish to.

2. Hire the correct professionals as necessary to deliver to platforms as diverse as print, e-book, and audio.

_____

_____

_____

_____

_____

_____

_____

_____

_____

_____

_____

Marketing, Distribution, and PR

Industry Best Practices

1. Perform a final, comprehensive quality check before production.

2. Ensure book is correctly produced on all platforms and/or formats.

3. Implement and tune your marketing and distribution plan.
   Follow up with finding and creating PR opportunities.

4. Track sales and tune your marketing plan further, based on results.

Once your book is published, you might think your work is over, that it's time to sit back and track sales. That would be nice, but there remains a lot of work to be done in the areas of marketing, distribution, and PR if you want your book to succeed. Of course, few authors are experts in the sales side of publishing, and this is where Izzard can help share the wisdom gained from experience.

Marketing

Leave little to chance—create a marketing plan and stick to it. Creating demand with readers is the best way to take advantage of a vast distribution network. On the flip side, a great marketing plan without distribution leads to frustrated fans who are not able to buy your book. Marketing and distribution go hand in hand.

Distribution

Distribution is fairly straightforward: Have your book available in as many formats and stores as possible. Give your readers the format they want to read.

An important part of distribution is deciding on the price of your book. Fiction and nonfiction have different pricing structures. Have you ever gone to buy an e-book online and thought, "That's too expensive!" and then noticed an advisory stating that the price was set by the publisher? An advantage of collaborative publishing with Izzard is that you can set your own price point.

For independent authors pricing print books is fairly straightforward. Typically, nonfiction retails for around $24.95 for a 325-page paperback book, and fiction is priced at about $16.95 for a 325-page paperback book. Some fiction titles can have a higher retail price. Historical fiction books are included in this small category, as they generally have the "value added" of great historical research entwined with an equally great story.

E-books can be a bit more complicated to price, though collaborative and self-published books tend to hit their maximum price at $9.99. But there is much to consider. For instance, did you know that when distributing on Amazon, a $0.99 price point generates only a 35% royalty instead of the roughly 70% royalty generated by a $2.99 price point? This little secret can increase your share by 100%! Always consider your available royalty when determining the price of your book. Izzard's experts can help you find the price point that will generate the most revenue for you, while not pricing yourself out of your own market.

PR

Once your book is on the market, don't give up on it. Continue to track its sales, noting where and when the most sales occur, especially in relation to any marketing efforts you are making. Continue to collect reviews, and showcase the best of them. Keep looking for ways to promote your book to those most likely to want it.

Planning Well

There is no substitute for having a good marketing plan that is robust and solid and will help you accomplish your ultimate goals. With experience gained from our successes, Izzard will work with you on your marketing plan, assisting you in streamlining and focusing it. We are also often able to identify advertising and PR venues that you might not have thought of, which have worked in the past for some of our most successful titles.

To create an effective marketing plan, it's important to start by revisiting your goals for the book. Are you hoping to get a message to a certain group of people? Are you working to dovetail the book with other online activities, such as a blog or newsfeed? Going back to your original worksheet, and with all the knowledge you've gained throughout this process, now is a good time to restate your goals, incorporating any adjustments or changes that you might have gained from acquiring a more thorough knowledge of the process: _____

_____

_____

_____

Going back to your earlier work, in what formats do you plan to publish (distribute) your book?

_____

_____

Now, let's look at your plan. In general terms, what are your plans to market your book? _____

_____

_____

What stands out about you and your book? Consider such things as groups with whom your book is likely to resonate. A religious-themed or politically themed book could be readily promoted by your church or local political organizations. Be creative! _____

_____

_____

_____

_____

_____

_____

Some ideas for marketing and PR:

Are you going to do a social media campaign?

☐ Yes   ☐ No

If yes, which social media sites do you think will be most productive? (While Facebook and Twitter are the most obvious choices, don't forget other social media outlets, like YouTube, LinkedIn, Ello, Pinterest, Instagram, Vimeo, Google+, etc.) Some social media outlets, such as Facebook, offer advertising options as part of the application. Also consider audio clips from your audiobook for a YouTube campaign.

_____

_____

_____

_____

_____

_____

_____

_____

Do you plan to consult with a PR agency that could possibly help get your book on TV or radio segments?

☐ Yes   ☐ No

If you have an agency in mind, put their company name here: _____

_____

Are you considering a blog?

☐ Yes   ☐ No

Blogs can help you create a mailing list. In fact, starting with friends and family, you can start compiling a mailing list now. Do you have a mailing list you can build on?

☐ Yes   ☐ No

Are you considering a book and/or speaking tour?

☐ Yes   ☐ No

Have you looked into the cost of local radio advertising?

☐ Yes   ☐ No

Have you looked into targeted and non-targeted online advertising?

☐ Yes   ☐ No

Have you considered whether you might be appropriate as a guest on a local (or national) TV or radio show?   ☐ Yes   ☐ No

If yes, which ones? _____

_____

_____

_____

Is it possible that a local organization, such as your church or chamber of commerce, would have an interest in helping you promote your book—for instance, if your book mentions the town or a local business?

☐ Yes   ☐ No

Keeping Track

Once your book is on the market, you will want to track sales. There are many tools for doing this, and many include analytical tools to help you fine-tune your PR as time passes. Here, we offer a simple tracking table and encourage you to use this or another tracker when your book goes to market. Use the information to improve and adjust your marketing efforts.

Time Frame	Number Sold	Up or Down By	Marketing Strategies in Use
Day 1			
Day 2			
Day 3			
Day 4			
Day 5			
Day 6			
Day 7			
WEEK 1			
Day 8			
Day 9			
Day 10			
Day 11			
Day 12			
Day 13			
Day 14			
WEEK 2			
WEEK 3			
WEEK 4			
MONTH 1			
WEEK 5			

Time Frame	Number Sold	Up or Down By	Marketing Strategies in Use
WEEK 6			
WEEK 7			
WEEK 8			
MONTH 2			
WEEK 9			
WEEK 10			
WEEK 11			
WEEK 12			
MONTH 3			
MONTH 4			
MONTH 5			
MONTH 6			
MONTH 7			
MONTH 8			
MONTH 9			
MONTH 10			
MONTH 11			
MONTH 12			

My Action Plan

1. Arrange for a thorough quality check prior to production.

2. Review produced book in all platforms and/or formats to ensure integrity.

3. Distribute your book and implement your marketing plan.

4. Identify PR opportunities such as local radio shows or events that may be relevant to the content of your book.

_____

_____

_____

_____

_____

_____

_____

_____

_____

_____

Specialty Markets

Industry Best Practices

1. Each type of specialty book has best practices specific to its needs, which professionals at Izzard Ink can identify.

There are types of books that require special treatment, and there are genres of books that have special markets on which you can capitalize.

Christian/Religious Publishing

For instance, Christian publishing is a growing market, and if your book touches on subjects of interest particular to Christians, or tells a story in which Christianity is part of the plot or action, remember that this can work in your favor by providing you with a preselected potential audience. Don't worry about getting pigeonholed—success in one market is actually a help in succeeding in another. Look at the Left Behind series. These books started out in the Christian book marketplace, but rapidly became crossover hits and were even picked up for movies. And the Christian-themed Chronicles of Narnia series, by C.S. Lewis, are among the most widely loved books of all time. If you have a niche, don't look at it as limiting; look at it as a ready-made audience and a possible springboard to greater success.

There are specialty markets for non-Christian religious and spiritual books as well. This kind of focus can give you a preselected audience for which advertising may be targeted on services such as Facebook, Google, radio, and printed media.

Fundamentally, though, publishing a book with a Christian or other religious theme is not significantly different from publishing any other book. Within Christian publishing, you will have the same subgenres you have elsewhere: religious, fiction, fantasy, dystopian, children's, young adult, mystery, romance, and so on.

Cookbooks

Some types of books, however, cannot be produced in the same way with the same success. Cookbooks, for example, need very specific layouts or a creative approach to flowing text. More often than not, they contain illustrations or photographs, and those illustrations must enhance the appearance of the food, not detract from it. Ingredient lists must be clear and easy to follow. Cooking instructions must be tested, as well as being clear and easy to follow. Layout is generally very important for cookbooks.

Bringing a cookbook to an electronic format is challenging but offers more options than bringing one to print. In print, though the layout may need work, once it is done, it is done, and one can expect the printed version to look as expected. In e-book format, where the user may have changed the type size and font, reflow could be an issue. You might consider a fixed layout, or you might consider innovative ideas for presenting cookbook content. The electronic format also allows you to provide creative links that may make your cookbook even more appealing—links to provide information about ingredients, or even where to order certain unusual items. Cookbooks are a good place for your personal creativity and innovation to work wonders!

Coffee-Table Books

A coffee-table book is an oversized, most often hardcover book intended for display on a table or a location where it is available to guests to spark conversation. The subject matter tends to be nonfiction and based on photos, in order to be skimmed or appreciated quickly by guests. Usually, the content is meant to be read and understood by a general audience, taking a broad view of subjects in captions and small blocks of text, instead of a deeper exploration. The subjects can cover broad, visually appealing territory such as art, pets, wildlife, architecture, history, and science.

Coffee-table books are often gift books, and appearance is very important. Cover design, as important as it is for all books, can be the make or break of a coffee-table book. Both the visual appeal of the front cover and the hook to the content on the back cover are absolutely critical in selling books such as these. In addition, coffee-table books are not cheap to produce, so they can't be cheap to sell. Work closely with your Izzard project manager to ensure the right balance between investment and sale price.

As coffee-table books are intended to be printed, and usually rich in illustrations and photos, you will want to have professionals ensuring that your graphics are faithfully reproduced and rights-cleared. Coffee-table books are often released in time to be bought as Christmas and holiday gifts, and some can become very popular. The list of the best coffee-table books at Goodreads.com includes *National Geographic: The Photographs*, edited by Leah Bendavid-Val; *The Art Book*, by Phaidon Press; *Ansel Adams: 400 Photographs*, by Ansel Adams; *Los Angeles: Portrait of a City*, edited by Jim Heimann; and *Diane Arbus: Revelations*, by Diane Arbus.

Children's Books

Children's books are another complex area, with subgenres and frequent special needs, such as fixed-layout requirements. It is also a particularly difficult market to break into. While upwards of twenty thousand children's books are published in the U.S. each year, that number is dwarfed by the number of manuscripts submitted. In addition, many publishers will not consider a book submitted with illustrations because they have their own stable of illustrators. When they get your manuscript, stripped of the art you or your talented colleague supplied, it may look considerably less appealing than it would have looked with all its pictures. If you are trying to publish traditionally, your illustrations probably won't be welcome. And yet to you, the illustrations may be a crucial part of what you feel makes the book attractive. In this case, having control over the publishing process can really work in your favor, to ensure that the product is what you envisioned.

In the world of traditional publishing, sadly, your children's book may not even be seen by the lowliest of slush readers before getting rejected. Rather than let this discourage you, remember that collaborative publishing with Izzard means you are no longer at the mercy of swamped, frustrated editors. You have control over the publication, illustration, distribution, and marketing of your book. Using the marketing techniques discussed before—finding that special selling point of your book and identifying the group that will most readily respond to it—you have the opportunity to find success on your own terms.

Following is a list of book genres that can be problematic or may need special care—but which are also likely to have a good, strong market you can capitalize on.

Place a check mark next to any category and/or genre that can apply to your book.

☐ Religious/spiritual

☐ Christian

☐ Subgenre: _____

☐ Judaica

☐ Subgenre: _____

☐ Other: _____

☐ Coffee-table book

☐ Cookbook

☐ Humor

☐ Language teaching

☐ Travelogue

☐ Children's book

   ☐ Subgenre: _____

☐ Coloring book

☐ Science/medical

☐ Technical with computer code

☐ Drama/screenplay

☐ Printed full color (four color, five color, six color)

Printed with spot color (usually black with one or two colored inks)

☐ Other

My Action Plan

1. Determine whether your book can be considered a "specialty" book.

2. Research what markets exist that are specific to your book type.

3. Identify how best to market your book in that specialized area.

_____

_____

_____

_____

_____

_____

_____

_____

_____

_____

ABOUT THE AUTHOR

As a multifaceted publishing visionary, Tim McConnehey specializes in the publishing of eBooks through his company, Izzard Ink Publishing.

And when he says multifaceted, he means it! Tim directs eight teams covering every facet of publishing: finance, distribution, marketing, website development, art, public relations, cover and interior design, audiobook production, editing, and copyright.

A solid leader, McConnehey has an outstanding record of growing market share, by continuously energizing and positively influencing team members to deliver solutions that not only improve productivity but deliver bottom-line results.

Through his background in corporate training, business management, and business development, Tim acquired extensive experience in client service. And as someone who is never satisfied with doing things the way they have always been done, he came up with the idea of creating Izzard Ink Publishing after reading an article about eBooks in *The Wall Street Journal*.

Izzard Ink Publishing has now grown from that initial idea to a business that has sold over 300,000 books and has a client list that has sold over 45 million books – all accomplished by delivering exceptional personalized client service and working with the best people in publishing.

Through McConnehey's promotion and marketing of their books, Izzard's authors have been featured on Fox News, C-Span's Book TV, *The New York Times, The Washington Post*, and other publications throughout the country.

McConnehey has a Bachelor of Arts in International Business, from Westminster College in Salt Lake City, and lives in Salt Lake City, Utah with his wife Wendy and their four children. When he does get the chance to get away, he loves to restore old cars and motorcycles.